MW01205387

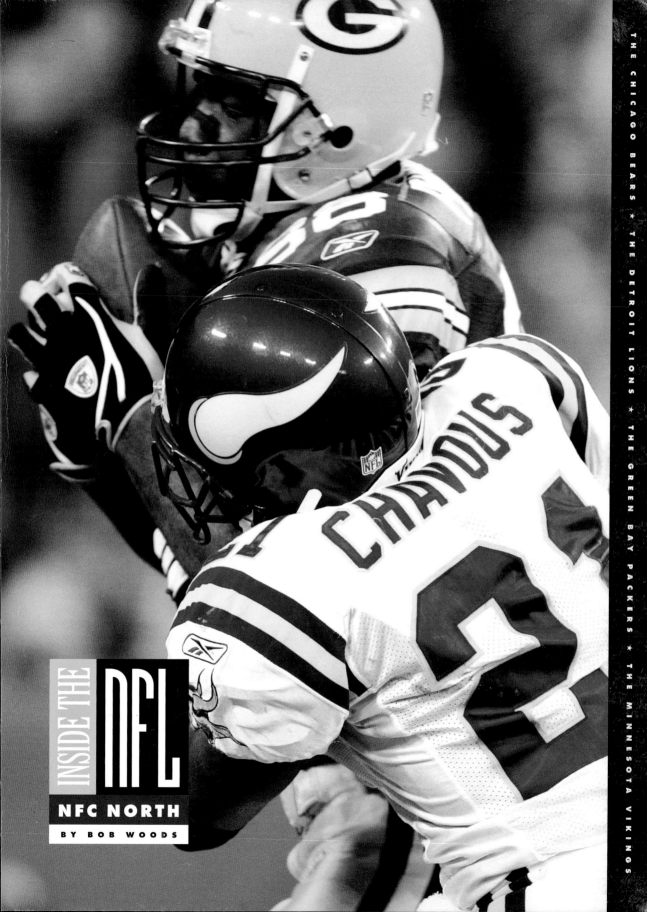

INSIDE THE **NFL**

NFC North

BY BOB WOODS

LIBRARY OF CONGRESS CATALOGING-IN-PUBLICATION DATA

Woods, Bob.
  NFC North / by Bob Woods.
    p. cm. — (Inside the NFL)
  Includes bibliographical references and index.
  ISBN 1-59296-513-X (library bound : alk. paper) 1. National Football League—
History—Juvenile literature. 2. Football—United States—History—Juvenile literature.
I. Title: National Football Conference North. II. Title. III. Series.
  GV955.5.N35W67 2006
  796.332'64'0973—dc22   2005004800

ACKNOWLEDGEMENTS

The Child's World®: Mary Berendes, Publishing Director

Editorial Directions, Inc.: Russell Primm, Editorial Director and Line Editor; Matt
Messbarger, Project Editor; Elizabeth K. Martin, Assistant Editor; Olivia Nellums,
Editorial Assistant; Susan Hindman, Copy Editor; Susan Ashley, Beth Franken,
Proofreaders; Kevin Cunningham, Fact Checker; Tim Griffin/IndexServ, Indexer;
James Buckley Jr., Photo Researcher and Selector

The Design Lab: Kathleen Petelinsek, Design and Page Production

Photos: Cover: Nam Y. Huh/AP
AP: 25; Brian Bahr/Getty: 41; Bettmann/Corbis: 7, 8, 10, 16, 18, 26, 34, 37;
Jonathan Daniel/Getty: 1, 2, 11, 14; Morry Gash/AP: 28; Annie Griffiths Belt/
Corbis: 36; Scott Halleran/Getty: 22; Rick Stewart/Getty: 20; Matthew Stockman:
32; Sports Gallery/Al Messerschmidt: 12, 21, 30, 35, 38

TABLE OF CONTENTS

Published in the United States of America by
The Child's World® • PO Box 326
Chanhassen, MN 55317-0326
800-599-READ • www.childsworld.com

The
Child's
World

INTRODUCTION

CHICAGO BEARS

Year Founded: 1920

Home Stadium:
Soldier Field

Year Stadium
Opened: 2003*

Team Colors:
Blue and orange

* *Renovated; original Soldier Field opened 1924*

DETROIT LIONS

Year Founded: 1930

Home Stadium:
Ford Field

Year Stadium
Opened: 2002

Team Colors: Silver and blue

In 1920, the American Professional Football Association (APFA) was founded in Canton, Ohio. Two years later, that name was changed to the National Football League (NFL). In the beginning, there were 14 teams. Among them was one in the middle of Illinois called the Decatur Staleys.

The Staleys moved north to Chicago in 1921, and a season later became the Bears. Also in 1921, the Green Bay Packers joined the APFA. In 1930, Ohio's Portsmouth Spartans entered the league, and in 1934, they motored to Detroit as the Lions. It wasn't until 1961 that the Minnesota Vikings sailed into Minneapolis.

Eventually, those four teams, plus the Tampa Bay Buccaneers, would rock and sock each other twice every season in the Central Division of the National Football Conference (NFC). Fans know it as the "Black and Blue Division." In 2002, the NFL reorganized, and now the Bears, Lions, Packers, and Vikings make up the NFC North.

Seem like a confusing combination of *Who's Who* and *Where's Waldo?* Don't worry, there won't be a test. And now that we've got our dates straight and located everyone, get ready to take a closer look at these famous franchises and their colorful characters.

For instance, take George Halas, who helped make the Bears into one of the NFL's most legendary teams. Where else but Chicago will you find a "Refrigerator" who made tackles and scored touchdowns?

The Lions roared through the 1950s, winning back-to-back championships, but haven't tasted much success lately. However, they still provide tasty entertainment on a certain Thursday in November that fans across the country are thankful to share.

The Packers have a homegrown story that could be the tale of a small town's high school football team. Yet Green Bay has produced legendary figures, such as Vince Lombardi, Bart Starr, and Brett Favre.

The Vikings, despite their late start in NFL life, caught up quite nicely with the Halases and the Favres. In fact, since 1961 only the Dallas Cowboys have made more playoff appearances than the Vikings.

So strap on your pads, lace up your cleats, and tighten your chinstrap. We're gonna tackle the "Black and Blue Division." We promise, though, it won't leave any bruises.

GREENBAY PACKERS

Year Founded: 1921

Home Stadium: Lambeau Field

Year Stadium Opened: 2003*

Team Colors: Green and gold

* Renovated; original Lambeau Field opened 1957

MINNESOTA VIKINGS

Year Founded: 1961

Home Stadium: Hubert H. Humphrey Metrodome

Year Stadium Opened: 1982

Team Colors: Purple and gold

CHAPTER ONE

THE CHICAGO BEARS

Before they were Bears, they were Staleys. Thank goodness someone changed the name. Could you imagine calling Bronko Nagurski or Dick Butkus or Brian Urlacher a Staley? And what the heck is a *Staley,* anyhow?

Actually, Staley is a who. Back in 1920, A. E. Staley owned a company in Decatur, Illinois, called the Staley Starch Works. He asked his new recreational director, George Halas, to organize and coach a company football team. The team was called—you guessed it—the Decatur Staleys.

Halas did such a terrific job that in 1921 his boss gave him the team, plus permission to move it to Chicago. Because the Staleys played home games in Cubs Park, home of the Chicago Cubs baseball team, a year later Halas dubbed his guys the Bears.

Right from the start, Halas's team—which he also played on until 1929—was good. Their first season, they won 10 games, lost one, and tied two. They would have captured the first APFA champion-

In 1985, the Bears' rap hit, the "Super Bowl Shuffle" was the first single to sell more than 1 million copies without cracking Billboard's Top 40 (it reached number 41).

George Halas gets a lift after the Bears' title in 1940.

ship, except the 13 other owners awarded it to the undefeated Akron Pros (8–0–3).

The Staleys won the 1921 NFL championship and finished second the next three seasons. In 1925, the Bears signed one of the NFL's first superstars, Red Grange. A gifted runner, the "Galloping Ghost" also

The Bears won the first official NFL Championship Game, in 1933, defeating the New York Giants, 23–21.

Bronko Nagurski was a force on offense and defense.

played defense. He drew huge crowds everywhere, which increased the NFL's popularity.

The Bears fielded other greats during that era. Paddy Driscoll could run, pass, catch, and particularly kick the football. His specialty, the **dropkick,** won many games. Bronko Nagurski, a rugged fullback and linebacker, powered the team to consecutive NFL championships in 1932 and 1933. The following year, his sensational blocking was his best weapon. Nagurski paved the way for Beattie Feathers to become the league's first 1,000-yard rusher (1,004). The Bears went undefeated, 13–0.

They literally slipped up in the NFL title game, though, against the New York Giants in 1934. Playing on an ice-covered field at New York's Polo Grounds, the Bears led at halftime, 10–3. In the second half, the Giants switched from cleats to basketball shoes for better traction. New York rallied to win "The Sneakers Game," 30–13.

The strong throwing arm of future Hall of Famer Sid Luckman carried Chicago to an 8–3 season in 1940. They wiped out the Washington Redskins, 73–0, in the championship game. That remains the most lopsided game in NFL history.

It was also the first of the Bears' four straight trips to the title game; they were champs again in 1941, 1943, and 1946.

Another generation of stars came out in the 1960s. They helped the team win it all in 1963. Tight end Mike Ditka was a sure-handed receiver and a hard-nosed blocker. Dick Butkus often is considered the best middle linebacker ever. Later, running back Gale Sayers scored 22 touchdowns as a rookie in 1965—including six in one game! These three players were the core of the team in 1967, the last year Halas coached.

Because of severe weather, the Bears played Portsmouth in the decisive game for the 1932 NFL title indoors at Chicago Stadium on an 80-yard field. The Bears won 9–0.

Gale Sayers was an instant star in 1965.

For their larger-than-life performances, the Bears earned the nickname Monsters of the Midway. That's a reference to the city's Midway Plaisance Park.

Over the next decade, the Bears basically went into hibernation. They didn't have a winning season again until 1977, when they were a **wild-card** team. They got that far in 1979, too, but both times were ousted in the first game.

The year before Halas died, in 1983, he brought Ditka back to coach the Bears. By 1985, "Iron Mike" had forged a team in his own image: tough, in-your-

When Walter Payton retired in 1987, he was the NFL's all-time leading rusher.

Brian Urlacher carries on the Bears' tradition as linebacker.

George "Papa Bear" Halas retired in 1967, with 40 seasons of coaching and a then-record 324 career wins to his credit.

face defense; run-oriented, grind-it-out offense. The stars were running back Walter Payton, linebacker Mike Singletary, and 300-pound (136-kilogram) defensive tackle William "Refrigerator" Perry. The Bears' fearsome "46" defense was designed to stuff the run and blitz the quarterback. Sometimes they stacked eight pass rushers near the **line of scrimmage.**

Chicago went 15–1 that season, then blanked the Giants (21–0) and the Rams (24–0) in the play-offs. In Super Bowl XX, they stomped the New England Patriots 46–10. Their win included a one-yard touchdown dive by the "Fridge," who lined up as a fullback.

The Bears remained Central Division champs the next three years, but saw only one playoff victory in that span. They were up and down in the early 1990s, before tailing off in the latter half under the team's 12th head coach, Dick Jauron.

Following a dismal 2000 season (5–11), Chicago caught magic in 2001. Consider their back-to-back miracle wins against San Francisco and Cleveland. In both games, the Bears rallied from big deficits. Twice, safety Mike Brown returned an interception for a touchdown. They finished the regular season 13–3 behind a typically tough defense, starring middle linebacker Brian Urlacher, and an efficient offense. Yet the Bears fell to the Philadelphia Eagles in the first game of the playoffs.

They fell back to Earth in 2002. They played at the University of Illinois stadium in Champaign while Soldier Field was being **renovated.** Chicago stumbled to a 4–12 finish. When the Bears' new stadium opened, their luck did not change. Five losses in the first six games in 2003 doomed Jauron, who was let go at the end of a 7–9 season. Lovie Smith, the man who built aggressive defenses as the coordinator in Tampa Bay and St. Louis, was hired to replace him.

Gale Sayers, who was known as the "Kansas Comet," had the short-est career (seven seasons) of any member of the Pro Football Hall of Fame.

Lovie Smith took over as head coach in 2004.

Walter Payton not only is the most prolific runner in Bears' history (16,726 yards), but he also holds the club record for the most receptions (492).

Smith's influence was evident from the start. Chicago featured a ball-hawking defense and improved special-teams play in 2004. And though the offense faltered and the Bears won just five games, they showed enough promise to give their fans hope for 2005 . . . and beyond.

CHAPTER TWO

THE DETROIT LIONS

Like Chicago's Bears, Detroit's Lions began their NFL life elsewhere as a "town team." Many of the league's early franchises were located in small midwestern communities, such as the Canton (Ohio) Bulldogs, the Decatur (Illinois) Staleys, the Muncie (Indiana) Flyers, the Rochester (Minnesota) Jeffersons, and the Portsmouth (Ohio) Spartans.

The Spartans entered the NFL in 1930, right at the beginning of the Great Depression. For three seasons, the team did well on the field, but bombed at the box office and fell deep into debt. George Richards, a Detroit radio executive, bought the Spartans in 1934, moved them to the "Motor City," and renamed them the Lions.

Some solid players came along, though none better than Dutch Clark. An All-NFL quarterback, he also ran the ball, kicked, and played defensive back. Clark propelled Detroit's new team to victory in its first 10 games. But by losing the final three, the Lions finished in second place.

On November 1, 2000, Ford Field was chosen to host Super Bowl XL, on February 5, 2006.

15

This vintage photo shows the Lions practicing in 1936.

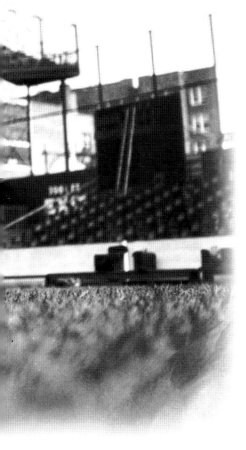

Two of those losses were to their Western Division rivals, the Bears. The first came on Thanksgiving, which began an NFL tradition of the Lions hosting a Turkey Day game every year. The most famous one occurred in 1962 against the Packers, who arrived at Tiger Stadium with a perfect 10–0 record. They left with their only loss of that season. The Lions' "Fearsome Foursome"—Darris McCord, Alex Karras, Roger Brown, and Sam Williams—sacked Bart Starr 11 times in a 26–14 Detroit victory.

The Lions played fearlessly in 1935 and clawed their way to the franchise's first NFL championship with a strong running game. Three Lions were among the NFL's top five rushers: Ernie Caddell, Clark, and Bill Shepherd.

The team posted winning records from 1936 to 1939, but only two over the next 10 seasons. Still, they fielded some memorable players, including a pair of

Cornerback Dick Lane was tagged "Night Train" during his rookie season with the Los Angeles Rams in 1952. He couldn't stop listening to Buddy Morrow's new hit song of the same name.

Joe Schmidt (No. 56) was a perennial all-pro linebacker.

The Lions reached the 1957 title game against Cleveland by rallying from a 27–7 third-quarter deficit to beat San Francisco 31–27 in a conference playoff.

Hall of Famers: halfback Bill Dudley and center-line-backer Alex Wojciechowicz. There was also Byron "Whizzer" White, a "triple threat" (passing, rushing, punting). He stayed only two seasons and eventually became a U.S. supreme court justice.

The 1950s were fabulous for the Lions. The team was loaded with stars. On offense were quarterback Bobby Layne, running back Doak Walker, and guard-tackle Lou Creekmur. The defense was led by safety Jack Christiansen. The quartet is now enshrined in the Pro Football Hall of Fame. During the decade, Detroit won three NFL championships, in 1952, 1953, and 1957.

All three championships were gained in hard-fought title games against the tough Cleveland Browns. In the 1953 game, Layne engineered a nail-biting, game-winning drive in the final minutes. With 2:08 left, he connected with Jim Doran—who usually played defensive end—for a 33-yard touchdown to seal the 17–16 win.

The Lions assembled a ferocious defense in the early 1960s. The top players were Joe Schmidt, Yale Lary, and Dick "Night Train" Lane. However, that mighty crew couldn't quite overcome the powerful Packers. The Lions came in second to them three straight seasons, 1960 to 1962. In fact, from 1969 through 1975, a frustrated Detroit played the second-place "bridesmaid" role seven consecutive times. That final season also marked the team's move to the suburbs and the Pontiac Metropolitan Stadium.

The Lions finally got over the hump and won the NFC Central Division in 1983—only to lose a 24–23 heartbreaker to the 49ers in the first playoff game. During the 1988 season, after too many losing seasons, owner William Clay Ford (grandson of Henry Ford) named Wayne Fontes head coach. Fontes used a fast-paced, **run-and-shoot offense** that the Lions called the "Silver Stretch."

With superstar running back Barry Sanders and speedy wide receivers, Detroit streaked to a 12–4, division-winning season in

After his playing career ended, defensive tackle Alex Karras launched an acting career. His most famous role was in the 1974 motion-picture comedy *Blazing Saddles*.

Quarterback Erik Kramer and the Lions made it all the way to the NFC title game in 1991.

Wayne Fontes, who led the Lions from 1988 to 1996, won more games (67) than any other coach in club history. Unfortunately, he also lost the most (71).

1991. They lost the NFC Championship Game to the Redskins, the eventual Super Bowl XXVI winners.

The phenomenal Sanders—only 5 feet 8 inches (173 centimeters) tall and 200 pounds (91 kg)—piled up rushing yards throughout the 1990s. He was the NFL's leading rusher in 1990, 1994, 1996, and 1997. He captured his third rushing title with a dramatic, 175-yard outburst on the final Monday night of the

Few runners ever have been as elusive as Barry Sanders.

Young Roy Williams is a potential superstar wide receiver.

season in San Francisco. In 1997, Sanders became only the third runner in NFL history to rush for more than 2,000 yards (2,053) in a season. To the fans' dismay, he suddenly retired after the 1998 campaign.

The Lions returned to the playoffs six times during the 1990s, but only came away with a single victory. The new millennium has not been kind to the team, though. After a 9–7 finish in 2000, the Lions sank to 2–14 in 2001.

The franchise ushered in a new era in 2002 when it unveiled new Ford Field in downtown Detroit and introduced the No. 1 draft pick, quarterback Joey Harrington. They only won three games, but the Lions were right back where they started: in the heart of the city and of every loyal fan.

Now, they would like to return to where they haven't been since 1957: atop the NFL. In 2003, Detroit charged coach Steve Mariucci, who guided San Francisco to the playoffs four times in six seasons from 1997 to 2002, with that daunting task.

The Lions haven't made it back to the playoffs yet under Mariucci, but they did show significant improvement while bolting to a 4–2 start in 2004. The club fizzled after that, losing several close games down the stretch, but was encouraged enough by the play of youngsters such as rookie running back Kevin Jones and rookie wide receiver Roy Williams that the postseason may be just on the horizon.

CHAPTER THREE

THE GREEN BAY PACKERS

As a city, Green Bay, Wisconsin, hardly measures up to New York, Chicago, or any of the other 31 NFL cities. When it comes to football, though, there's no place like Green Bay. Just ask the "cheeseheads" who fill Lambeau Field to cheer on their beloved Packers.

Fortunately, those fans aren't called meatheads. After all, the team was founded by a local meat-packing company (Packers, get it?) in 1919. Two years later, they joined the NFL. Since then, the Packers have won more championships than any other NFL franchise (12).

Earl "Curly" Lambeau, who worked for the packing company, was the team's first coach. They did well throughout the 1920s, then in 1929, with a 12–0–1 record, won the first of three straight NFL championships.

Leaders of the original "Pack" were some of the game's earliest superstars. These players included tailback Arnie Herber, tackle Cal Hubbard, and Johnny "Blood" McNally. New blood arrived over the next few years, including fullback Clarke Hinkle and

> **The Packers first played on a couple of small fields in Green Bay, and then in 6,000-seat City Stadium beginning in 1925.**

Don Hutson was the first of the NFL's great pass catchers.

receiver Don Hutson. All of them are now in the Hall of Fame.

The Packers claimed another NFL title in 1936. They lost to the Giants in the 1938 championship game, but shut out New York a year later, 27–0, to earn the franchise's fifth title.

While a college player at Fordham, Vince Lombardi was one of the legendary "Seven Blocks of Granite."

Vince Lombardi's Packers won five NFL titles in the 1960s.

Green Bay bettered its New York rivals again in 1944. That title game was dominated by fullback Ted Fritsch. He scored both touchdowns in the Packers' 14–7 triumph. Then began a long drought. From 1945 to 1959, the Packers finished no better than

Don Hutson led the league in receiving in eight of his eleven seasons.

third place. Fortunately, better days lay ahead.

Vince Lombardi was hired as coach and **general manager** in 1959. He inherited a squad loaded with future Hall of Famers. The stars were quarterback Bart Starr, fullback Jim Taylor, halfback Paul Hornung, tackle Forrest Gregg, and center Jim Ringo. They went 7–5 Lombardi's first year—the team's first winning season since 1947.

The Packers lost the championship game in 1960, Lombardi's only playoff defeat. Taylor ran for 1,307 yards in 1961, and Green Bay won the West again. They shut out the Giants, 37–0, in the title game. After a 13–1 finish in 1962, the Pack edged New York, 16–7, for yet another championship.

In 1965, Baltimore and Green Bay ended with identical 10–3–1 records, forcing a playoff game. A Don Chandler field goal was the difference in a 13–10 Packers win. The title game was played on a cold, snow- and mud-drenched Lambeau Field. Green Bay held Cleveland's bruising fullback Jim Brown to 50 yards. Meanwhile, Taylor and Hornung combined to gain 201 yards, and the home team prevailed, 23–12.

Two more consecutive NFL championships netted trips to Super Bowls I and II to play the winners of the rival American Football League (AFL). In 1967, Green Bay scored three second-half touchdowns to topple the Kansas City Chiefs, 35–10. Super Bowl II, versus the Oakland Raiders, featured another second-half surge and Packers victory. Alas, that was Lombardi's last game in so-called "Titletown."

Despite the Packers' storied tradition, only four of their 14 coaches in history have posted winning records: Curly Lambeau, Vince Lombardi, Mike Holmgren, and Mike Sherman.

Quarterback Brett Favre made the Packers number one again in the 1990s.

Several coaches, including Starr and Gregg, tried—but failed—to rekindle the Lombardi magic. Except for playoff appearances in 1972 and 1982, the Packers were mediocre until the early 1990s. Head coach Mike Holmgren, an offensive guru from the 49ers, came to town in 1992, along with quarterback Brett Favre.

Super Bowl XXXI Most Valuable Player (MVP) Desmond Howard returned a kickoff 99 yards to seal the Green Bay victory.

Fearless in the **pocket,** the cannon-armed Favre and receiver Sterling Sharpe helped Green Bay to the playoffs in 1993. They won wild-card games that year and the next.

By 1995, a defense sparked by hulking defensive end Reggie White slammed the brakes on opponents. The 11–5 Packers dethroned the reigning NFL champion 49ers in the second playoff game. In the NFC title game against Dallas, however, they ran out of gas in the fourth quarter and lost.

The Pack was back in 1996, as

Ahman Green is a dual threat as a runner and pass catcher.

Reggie White, who played six of his 15 seasons with the Packers, finished his NFL career in 2000 as the league's all-time leader with 198 sacks.

Favre earned his second of three straight league MVP trophies. A dominant 13–3 regular season ended with a resounding 35–21 victory over New England in Super Bowl XXXI. It was Green Bay's first NFL title since 1967.

In 1997, the Packers defended their title in Super Bowl XXXII against the Broncos. Favre rallied his team in the second half, only to be thwarted by a late Denver touchdown that sealed a 31–24 win. Green Bay went 11–5 in 1998, but lost the wild-card game in the final seconds to the 49ers. Holmgren resigned and was replaced by Ray Rhodes, who lasted one season (8–8). Thus ended the Packers' six-year playoff streak.

In 2001, under new head coach Mike Sherman, Favre became the first NFL passer with 10 straight 3,000-yard seasons. Sherman directed the 12–4 Packers back to the playoffs. However, the valiant quarterback threw six interceptions in a divisional playoff game versus the Rams in a 45–17 defeat.

Sherman's troops marched to another 12–4 season in 2002. But history was not on the Packers' side. For the first time, they lost a playoff game at Lambeau—shocked by the Falcons, 27–7.

The Packers moved into refurbished Lambeau Field in 2003, but the new-look stadium produced the same results: another division championship. Then came a pair of heart-stoppers in the playoffs. In the opening round, cornerback Al Harris sent the home fans into a frenzy by returning an interception 52 yards for the game-winning touchdown in overtime against Seattle. But in the divisional playoffs a week later, the tables were turned when Favre was intercepted on Green Bay's first play in overtime, leading to the winning field goal by the Eagles.

At age 35 in 2004, Favre had one of his best seasons, passing for 4,088 yards and 30 touchdowns. Favre's passing, Ahman Green's running, and the emergence of Javon Walker as a big-play wide

Javon Walker is the latest big-play receiving threat for the Packers.

Green Bay is the only team to win three consecutive NFL titles—and the Packers have done it twice (1929–1931 and 1965–1967).

receiver helped put Green Bay atop the NFC North for the third time in the division's three years of existence.

Though the season ended with an upset loss to the Vikings in the opening round of the playoffs, the cheeseheads have every reason to believe that the NFL world will be calling Green Bay "Titletown" again before long.

CHAPTER FOUR

THE MINNESOTA VIKINGS

The Vikings' induction into the "Black and Blue Division" on September 17, 1961, left the Chicago Bears red-faced with embarrassment. The big, bad Bears had been in the league for 40 years already and had seven NFL championships under their shoulder pads.

That didn't matter to the Vikings, a mix of **expansion draft** veterans and raw rookies. One of them unexpectedly matured that Sunday afternoon. Quarterback Fran Tarkenton came off the bench and passed for four touchdowns and scrambled for another. The 37–13 victory upset Chicago, but thrilled the more than 32,000 Vikings fans who packed Metropolitan Stadium in Minneapolis.

Minnesota won only two more games during that inaugural season. Meanwhile, head coach Norm Van Brocklin was nurturing his young team. With Tarkenton under center, halfback Tommy Mason and fullback Bill Brown in the backfield, Paul Flatley at wide receiver, and Carl Eller at defensive end, the "Vikes" achieved their

Following his "people eating" days, Alan Page became a lawyer and eventually a Minnesota supreme court justice.

Hall of Fame safety Paul Krause, who played for the Vikings from 1968 to 1979, is the NFL's all-time leader with 81 career interceptions.

first winning season (8–5–1) in 1964.

But Van Brocklin and Tarkenton feuded, and both departed following the disappointing 1966 season (4–9–1). Down came Bud Grant, head coach of the **Canadian Football League**'s Winnipeg Blue Bombers, and up went the Vikings' fortunes. Grant developed a cast of talented rookies: defensive tackle Alan Page, wide receiver Gene Washington, running

Fran Tarkenton confounded opponents with his scrambling.

Stoic Bud Grant's expression rarely changed.

back Clint Jones, and defensive backs Bobby Bryant and Bob Grim. He also recruited quarterback Joe Kapp, his **signal caller** in Winnipeg.

Kapp and company captured the Central Division title in 1968, but lost to Baltimore in the Vikings' first postseason game. Minnesota ruled the "Black and Blue" in 1969, going 12–2, then won two home playoff games and met the Chiefs in Super Bowl IV. Despite being favored by two touchdowns, the Vikings got trounced, 23–7.

The NFL's revolving door brought Tarkenton back to Minnesota from the Giants in 1972, though

Bud Grant was a basketball and football star at the University of Minnesota before being drafted in 1950 by the old Minneapolis (now Los Angeles) Lakers and the Philadelphia Eagles. He played offensive and defensive end for the Eagles from 1951 to 1952.

the team only managed a .500 finish. They enjoyed a division-best 12–2 record in 1973, which began an incredible—if frustrating—six-year postseason streak. It started with the first of six straight Central Division titles, then a playoff run to Super Bowl VIII, which they lost to the Dolphins, 24–7.

Jim Marshall was an iron man at defensive end.

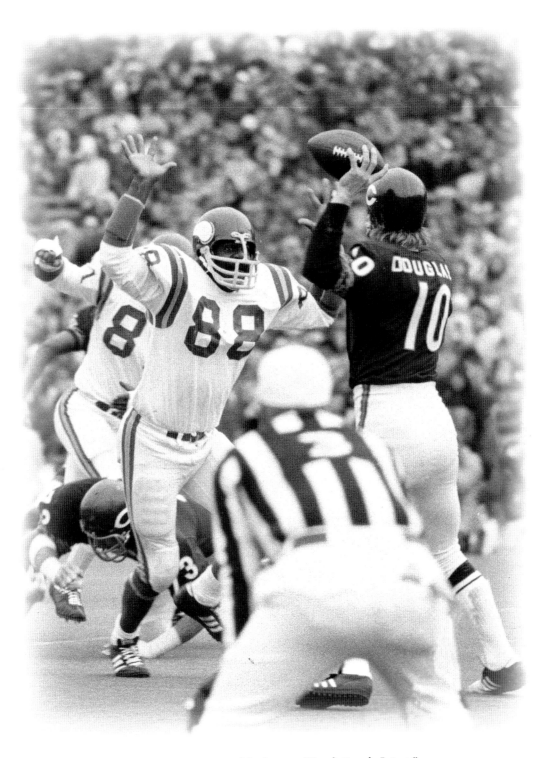

Alan Page was one of the famous "Purple People Eaters."

While in Minnesota from 1998 to 2004, Randy Moss
was one of the league's top receivers.

In 2001, Vikings
wide receiver Cris
Carter became only
the second player in
NFL history to catch
more than 1,000
career passes (Jerry
Rice was the first).

During that period, the defense's "Purple People
Eaters" devoured opponents. That nickname defined
Minnesota's ravenous **front four:** Eller, Page, Gary
Larsen, and Jim Marshall. Not huge, but uncom-
monly quick, they attacked the ball. Whether it was
sacking the quarterback, tackling a ball carrier for a
loss, or batting down a pass, they were relentless.

In 1974, Minnesota advanced to its third Super Bowl, only to be turned away this time by the Steelers. After another 12–2 season in 1975, the Vikings dropped their first playoff game to Dallas on a Roger Staubach 50-yard bomb to Drew Pearson with 24 seconds left. Grant guided his squad to a fourth Super Bowl in 1976, but they were beaten by the Oakland Raiders.

The Vikings returned to the playoffs the next two seasons, but failed to reach the Super Bowl. By then, too, the Purple People Eaters' reign of terror was over.

Following playoff runs in 1980 and 1982, Grant retired after the 1983 season—Minnesota's second in the Metrodome. The team slumped to 3–13 in 1984. Grant came back for the 1985 season, then turned over the reins to longtime assistant Jerry Burns.

Burns produced three playoff teams, the last during the 1989 season when the Vikings and the Cowboys pulled off a megadeal. Minnesota sent players and draft picks to Dallas for Heisman Trophy running back Herschel Walker. However, ill-suited to the Vikings's offense, he went to the Eagles two years later.

By the mid-1990s, Minnesota possessed a potent passing game. They obtained Oilers quarterback Warren Moon, who meshed with receivers Jake Reed, Qadry Ismail, and Cris Carter. Dennis Green, who replaced Burns in 1992, pushed the team to the playoffs his first three seasons but failed to win a postseason game.

In fact, their next playoff victory was a shocker against the Giants in 1997. Trailing 22–13 in the fourth quarter, Minnesota scored 10 points in 90 seconds for the miraculous win. They weren't as fortunate the following year, when they took an NFL-best 15–1 record into the playoffs. Apparently destined for Super Bowl XXXIII, they lost in overtime to Atlanta in the NFC title game.

A fresh generation of superstars powered the Vikings into the new century. Daunte Culpepper represents the new-age quarterback: big, powerful, mobile, and strong-armed. He's complemented by rangy receiver Randy Moss, whose leaping ability and elusiveness after a catch make the duo dynamic. Yet back-to-back postseason collapses in 1999 and 2000 were followed by two more losing seasons.

Under second-year coach Mike Tice (a former tight end for the club), the Vikings bounced back to win nine games in 2003. And though they were only 8–8 in 2004, they reached the playoffs for the first time in four years as a wild-card team.

Culpepper had one of the best seasons by a quarterback in NFL history that year, passing for 4,717 yards and 39 touchdowns while compiling a passer rating of 110.9, the fourth best ever. Moss, though hampered by injuries, still caught 13 touchdown passes, and Minnesota scored more points (405) than any other NFC team except Green Bay.

In seven years in Minnesota Randy Moss caught 574 passes, including 90 touchdowns. But he was traded to Oakland following the 2004 season.

Then, in the playoffs, the Vikings pulled off a shocker. Despite entering the game with 20 losses in their last 22 games played outdoors, the Vikings blasted the division-rival Packers 31–17. Culpepper passed for 284 yards and four touchdowns, including two to Moss, as Minnesota handed Green Bay only its second postseason loss ever at historic Lambeau field.

Quarterback Daunte Culpepper and the Vikings raced past the Packers in the 2004 playoffs.

The season ended a week later with a loss at eventual NFC-champion Philadelphia. But the Vikings had served notice that they were still one of the NFL's most explosive and exciting teams.

STAT STUFF

TEAM RECORDS

TEAM	ALL-TIME RECORD	NFL TITLES (MOST RECENT)	NUMBER OF TIMES IN PLAYOFFS	TOP COACH (WINS)
Chicago	646–474–42	9 (1985)	22	George Halas (324)
Detroit	473–520–32	4 (1957)	14	Wayne Fontes (67)
Green Bay	612–480–36	12 (1996)	23	Curly Lambeau (212)
Minnesota	362–291–9	1 (1969)	24	Bud Grant (168)

MEMBERS OF THE PRO FOOTBALL HALL OF FAME

MINNESOTA

PLAYER	POSITION	DATE INDUCTED
Dave Casper	Tight end	2002
Carl Eller	Defensive end	2004
Jim Finks	General Manager	1995
Bud Grant	Coach	1994
Paul Krause	Safety	1998
Jim Langer	Center	1987
Hugh McElhenny	Halfback	1970
Alan Page	Defensive Tackle	1988
Jan Stenerud	Kicker	1991
Fran Tarkenton	Quarterback	1986
Ron Yary	Tackle	2001

DETROIT

PLAYER	POSITION	DATE INDUCTED
Lem Barney	Cornerback	1992
Jack Christiansen	Defensive Back	1970
Earl (Dutch) Clark	Quarterback	1963
Lou Creekmur	Tackle/Guard	1996
Bill Dudley	Halfback	1966
Frank Gatski	Center	1985
John Henry Johnson	Fullback	1987
Dick (Night Train) Lane	Cornerback	1974
Yale Lary	Defensive Back	1979
Bobby Layne	Quarterback	1967
Ollie Matson	Halfback	1972
Hugh McElhenny	Halfback	1970
Barry Sanders	Running back	2004
Joe Schmidt	Linebacker	1973
Doak Walker	Halfback	1986
Alex Wojciechowicz	Center/Linebacker	1968

MEMBERS OF THE PRO FOOTBALL HALL OF FAME

CHICAGO

PLAYER	POSITION	DATE INDUCTED
Doug Atkins	Defensive End	1982
George Blanda	Quarterback/Kicker	1981
Dick Butkus	Linebacker	1979
Guy Chamberlin	End/Coach	1965
George Connor	Tackle	1975
Jimmy Conzelman	Quarterback/Coach	1964
Mike Ditka	Tight End	1988
John (Paddy) Driscoll	Quarterback	1965
Jim Finks	General Manager	1995
Dan Fortmann	Guard	1965
Bill George	Linebacker	1974
Harold (Red) Grange	Halfback	1963
George Halas	Coach/Owner	1963
Dan Hampton	Defensive End	2002
Ed Healey	Tackle	1964
Bill Hewitt	Wide Receiver	1971
Stan Jones	Guard/Defensive Tackle	1991
Walt Kiesling	Guard/Coach	1966
Bobby Layne	Quarterback	1967
Sid Luckman	Quarterback	1965
William Roy (Link) Lyman	Tackle	1964
George McAfee	Halfback	1966
George Musso	Guard	1982
Bronko Nagurski	Fullback	1963
Alan Page	Defensive tackle	1988
Walter Payton	Running Back	1993
Gale Sayers	Running Back	1977
Mike Singletary	Linebacker	1998
Joe Stydahar	Tackle	1967
George Trafton	Center	1964

GREEN BAY

PLAYER	POSITION	DATE INDUCTED
Herb Adderley	Cornerback	1980
Tony Canadeo	Halfback	1974
Willie Davis	Defensive End	1981
Len Ford	Defensive end	1976
Forrest Gregg	Tackle/Guard	1977
Todd Hendricks	Linebacker	1990
Arnie Herber	Quarterback	1966
Clarke Hinkle	Fullback	1964
Paul Hornung	Halfback	1986
Robert (Cal) Hubbard	Tackle	1963
Don Hutson	Wide Receiver	1963
Henry Jordan	Defensive Tackle	1995
Walt Kiesling	Guard/Coach	1966
Earl (Curly) Lambeau	Coach	1963
James Lofton	Wide Receiver	2003
Vince Lombardi	Coach	1971
John (Blood) McNally	Halfback	1963
Mike Michalske	Guard	1964
Ray Nitschke	Middle Linebacker	1978
Jim Ringo	Center	1981
Bart Starr	Quarterback	1977
Jan Stenerud	Kicker	1991
Jim Taylor	Fullback	1976
Emlen Tunnell	Safety	1967
Willie Wood	Safety	1989

MORE STAT STUFF

N F C   N O R T H   C A R E E R   L E A D E R S   (T H R O U G H   2 0 0 4)

CHICAGO

CATEGORY	NAME (YEARS WITH TEAM)	TOTAL
Rushing	Walter Payton (1975-1987)	16,726
Passing yards	Sid Luckman (1939-1950)	14,686
Touchdown passes	Sid Luckman (1939-1950)	137
Receptions	Walter Payton (1975-1987)	492
Touchdowns	Walter Payton (1975-1987)	125
Scoring	Kevin Butler (1985-1995)	1,116

DETROIT

CATEGORY	NAME (YEARS WITH TEAM)	TOTAL
Rushing	Barry Sanders (1989-1998)	15,269
Passing yards	Bobby Layne (1950-1958)	15,710
Touchdown passes	Bobby Layne (1950-1958)	118
Receptions	Herman Moore (1991-2001)	670
Touchdowns	Barry Sanders (1989-1998)	109
Scoring	Jason Hanson (1992-2004)	1,336

GREEN BAY

CATEGORY	NAME (YEARS WITH TEAM)	TOTAL
Rushing	Jim Taylor (1958-1966)	8,207
Passing yards	Brett Favre (1992-2004)	49,734
Touchdown passes	Brett Favre (1992-2004)	376
Receptions	Sterling Sharpe (1988-1994)	595
Touchdowns	Don Hutson (1935-1945)	105
Scoring	Ryan Longwell (1997-2004)	964

MINNESOTA

CATEGORY	NAME (YEARS WITH TEAM)	TOTAL
Rushing	Robert Smith (1993-2000)	6,818
Passing yards	Fran Tarkenton (1961-66, 1972-78)	33,098
Touchdown passes	Fran Tarkenton (1961-66, 1972-78)	239
Receptions	Cris Carter (1990-2001)	1,004
Touchdowns	Cris Carter (1990-2001)	110
Scoring	Fred Cox (1963-1977)	1,365

GLOSSARY

Canadian Football League—the group of teams that play in various cities in Canada; this league is separate from the NFL and has slightly different rules and uses a larger field

dropkick—a kick made by dropping the ball straight down and striking it just as it hits the ground; though still legal, it is never used in the NFL

expansion draft—when a new team enters the NFL, older teams let the new team choose players from their rosters

front four—the defensive line

general manager—a person who runs the football team away from the field, helping choose players and organizing the business

line of scrimmage—the point on the field from which a play begins

pocket—the space around a quarterback created by blockers as he tries to pass

renovated—fixed up, renewed, improved

run-and-shoot offense—a strategy that uses many short passes, quick runs, and few huddles

signal caller—a nickname for a quarterback

wild-card—a team that makes the playoffs without winning a division title

TIME LINE

1920   American Professional Football Association founded, with Decatur Staleys (later Chicago Bears) as one of its first members; league changed its name to the National Football League in 1922

1921   Green Bay Packers join league; Staleys win title

1929   Packers win first of three straight league titles

1933   Bears win first NFL Championship Game over New York Giants

1934   Portsmouth team moves to Detroit and takes the name Lions

1940   Bears set a record by defeating Washington 73–0 to win NFL championship; they also won the league in 1941, 1943, and 1946

1952   Detroit wins first of two straight league titles; they would win again in 1957

1961   Green Bay wins NFL championship, first of five it would win in the decade; Minnesota Vikings play first season in NFL, finishing 3–11

1966   Green Bay wins first AFL-NFL Championship Game, later called Super Bowl I; also would win in 1967

1969   Vikings earn berth in Super Bowl IV, first of four Super Bowls the team would play in and lose

1985   Chicago wins Super Bowl XX

1996   Green Bay wins Super Bowl XXXI; they would lose in Super Bowl XXXII the next season

FOR MORE INFORMATION ABOUT

THE NFC NORTH AND THE NFL

BOOKS

Buckley, James Jr. *Super Bowl Heroes.* New York: DK Publishing, 2000.

Buckley, James Jr., and Jerry Rice. *America's Greatest Game.* New York: Hyperion Books for Children, 1998.

Firsch, Aaron. *The History of the Chicago Bears.* Mankato, Minn.: Creative Education, 2005.

Firsch, Aaron. *The History of the Detroit Lions.* Mankato, Minn.: Creative Education, 2005.

Firsch, Aaron. *The History of the Minnesota Vikings.* Mankato, Minn.: Creative Education, 2005.

Grabowski, John. *The Minnesota Vikings.* San Diego: Lucent Books, 2003.

Gutman, Bill. *Brett Favre: Leader of the Pack.* Brookfield, Conn: Millbrook Press, 1998.

Koslow, Philip. *Walter Payton.* Broomall, Penn.: Chelsea House, 1994.

Molzahn, Arlene. *The Green Bay Packers.* Springfield, N.J.: Enslow Publishers, 1999.

Murray, Mike. *60 Years of Lions Football.* Dallas: Taylor Publishing, 1993.

Nichols, John. *The History of the Green Bay Packers.* Mankato, Minn.: Creative Education, 2005.

O'Shei, Tim. *The Chicago Bears Football Team (Great Sports Teams).* Springfield, N.J.: Enslow Publishers, 2001.

Whittingham, Richard. *The Chicago Bears: A 75-Year Celebration.* Dallas: Taylor Publishing, 1994.

ON THE WEB

Visit our home page for lots of links about the NFC North:

http://www.childsworld.com/links

Note to Parents, Teachers, and Librarians: We routinely verify our Web links to make sure they are safe, active sites—so encourage your readers to check them out!

INDEX

A B O U T   T H E   A U T H O R

Bob Woods is a freelance writer in Madison, Connecticut.
Over the past 20 years, his work has appeared in many
magazines, including *Sports Illustrated*. He has written books
for young readers about Barry Bonds, Shaquille O'Neal,
NASCAR history, and other sports topics.